CHILDREN MUST NOT Cry

AISHA KONATEH

AuthorHouse™ UK Ltd.
1663 Liberty Drive
Bloomington, IN 47403 USA
www.authorhouse.co.uk
Phone: 0800.197.4150

Published by AuthorHouse 02/28/2014

ISBN: 978-1-4918-9642-6 (sc)
*   978-1-4918-9643-3 (e)*

INTRODUCTION

THE CHILDREN MUST NOT CRY, This is a book that I picked from the bottom of my heart to ensure peace and stability in the world. I have not experience a lot, but have seen or heard the problems that people encounter in the struggle for peace through wars, conflicts and other problems. The saddest part of it is the life of children, they are vulnerable and needs help to survive.

I wrote this book not to cause problems, but to make peace between people of all areas. In life, it is hard when certain things happened, but truthfulness, patients and hard work is the weapon to fight evil.

It is a book that I wrote not to make people sad, but to give courage to the world for peace. This book may contain some stress flashing images or words of sympathy and am very sorry for any inconvenience.

Life is full of challenges that must be overcome through good to achieve good.

MY BIOGRAPHY

I am a Gambian by Nationality and currently staying at Leeds , UK. I am now studying at Leeds Technology College and doing a child care course to help, serve and strengthen the nature of childhood.

I graduated from a high school in the Gambia and a certificate holder in International relationships and politics, which I came with some distinctions, from Stratford College of Management, The Gambia.

I recently trained as a volunteer at Patient Health Champion [PHC] training to help the Community on issues pertaining to their health.

I belief every life is worth of living and deserves to be help.

DEDICATION

I dedicate this book to my parents and siblings.

I dedicate it to every parent or guardians, who struggle to achieve good life for their children.

I dedicate it to every child, who respect his parent and are struggling for their futures.

I dedicate it to every Government and organisations , who are working harder to develop the life of every child.

Last, but one I dedicate it to every parent or guardians, who are not playing their roles, I dedicate it to them, because I want them to work harder to achieve good for their children.

I dedicate it to the world, for the resolution of peace and unity among people of all areas.

TABLE OF CONTENTS

1. ROLE OF PARENTS.

Parents must respect and valued their children

A parent must be very caring to children.

They must provide basic needs for their children.

parents must not be violent against children.

They must make sure children are regular in school.

parents must also check the performance of their children in school.

parents must be vigilant to know the behavior of their children.

They must leave children to make decisions, If not contrary to good.

They must make sure children are protected.

They must also help their children to be clean and sound minded.

They must teach their children to be polite or have good attitudes.

AN ADVICE TO CHILDREN.

A child is born to be good.

Children must obey their parents.

Children must also respect their parents and other people.

Children must try to be educated and hardworking.

Children must also have good attitudes and learn to be grateful.

Children must not be violent.

They must not use abusive or bad languages.

They must be regular or punctual in school.

They must obey law and order.

They must not disturb their parents or guardians.

They must not steal or lie.

Children as a whole must not do anything bad.

CHILDREN BE HAPPY.

You are not a tree that stands without a parent or guardian.

You are not a flower that people put in their houses or gardens for decoration.

You are not a stature that stands straight only to be watched by people or remembered.

You are not a snake that stays in holes or grasses for living.

You are not an animal that stays in the bush or forest without a house to live or a school to attend.

You are not a Bahama grass that is use for playing football and other activities.

You are not a sand that people use to build houses, offices, industries or factories, warehouses and roads.

You are born to be special and live to be respected.

Children be happy and concentrate on good manners or behaviors to live a successful life. Politeness, self esteem, self reliance, focus and commitment are the best behaviors for every child. Be active to know your capacities and work on that to have a brighter future.

PARENTS MUST NOT ABANDON THEIR CHILDREN.

Parents are the most important people in every child's life. A girl child as well as boys are all born to be safe , this is the responsibility of every parent from every state. No matter how difficult life may be , these responsibilities must not be neglected or abandon.

Life is worth of living and every parent's help is needed to support the life of every child. Children cry out for help everyday and they need their parents to survive. They are the future leaders and that must be considered forever.

A child is only a child and knows nothing about success, but this is the responsibility of parents to pave the way for their children. Smile to your child as it is the best charity of the face. Make him or her your friend and teach them to understand the reality of life. Try as much as you can to eradicate evil from your child's life, abandon him not, never abuse him or make him afraid. Give him all support he needed and be a bodyguard to his life. Stand near him all times and be very firm. The live of children are very important and cannot be underestimated.

Child issues cannot be discuss without parents, this makes the role of parents important. Caring and the protecting of children is a priority for all parents and the world at large. The benefit of power can be shown through the help of children to attain liberty, equality, progress, peace and prosperity. Parents must give rights to their children and children must also know their limitations. The life of every child is important and must observe those legal rights to be safe. All children must have rights to three things, that is right to life, liberty and property. These are the greatest empowerments that every child needs to survive.

Every child is born to a family, whether known or unknown and parents must not abandon their children. Life is precious than every thing and must be protected in all ways. Children are human beings as well as any other person. The will of every child must be fully respected, when not contrary to good. Parents must help their children to learn, make good decisions, understanding the nature of humanity, knowing how to behave. example good body language, self reliance and being grateful in life.

A Parent is only a parent, they cannot take the role of their children and neither can a child take the role of their parents. They all have a role to play and these roles must be based on ethics and responsibilities. Let every child respect his parents and live comfortably in the society. These are realities that needs to be considered in life.

NO CHILD IS BORN USELESS.

A child can be a president or a prime minister, a Doctor, a Business man or woman, an architecture, an Engineer, a child career, a Banker, a Journalist, a Teacher, a Driver, a Pilot, a Farmer, a Soldier, a Policeman or woman, etc. I would like to say all, but I can't. Give chance to your children and always consider that none is born useless. it sometimes depends on the way a child is brought up. Every child is an attention seeker and needs help to be happy. Children are gifts from God and needs protection to be safe. Every life matters and the burden of hardship must not be bear.

The world gets more darker everyday, because of violence. Who is there to make it stop? there are many violence that children face everyday and the help of every parent is counted.

No child is born useless, If all parents put this in to consideration, then the world would be a paradise for every child. Good attitude, self esteem, religious tolerance, being good to people, give chance to others, understanding the nature of human beings, these are what brings the emergence of peace to every heart. Life is put in to the body not because of evil, but good. Children should not be tortured or punish for a purpose that is not genuine. If a child misbehaves does not mean he or she is evil, but needs help to see the way. All children needs parents to show them the straight path. No child is born to be useless. Support a child today for a good future and consider them as born to be safe.

Little steps are great steps, please help children to live happily and be a successful parents or guardians forever. Violence against children is out of hand and the world must protect the life of every child. There are many problems that affects children and among them are child trafficking, kidnapping, child labor, rape cases, abortions, unwanted pregnancy, drug abuse or trafficking, alcoholic, child prostitution, torturing and different types of punishments etc. These are some of the problems that affects children In all parts of the world. They are very rampant and some thing needs to be done to save the lives of children from calamities. Every person must be a policeman to save and protect the lives of children.

SAVE THE CHILDREN.

Generations has come and gone , because that is the destiny of life. All generations has come with their children. Now is the twenty first century and any child born on this generation will be termed as children of the twenty first century or the twenty first century born children. This is an ancient process and continues to be a modern one, in the sense that, since time in memorial women have being given birth till today. That is why child bearing is ancient and the same time modern. These makes children important in life. They are future leaders which there is no doubt. The coming of children to the world is a development and every development comes with success.

Save the children and protect them from harm. Be a bodyguard to protect children and your reward would one day be granted. Support them always and teach them to understand the world. Parents or guardians must redouble their efforts to bring peace to the lives of every child from every corner. Talk to them always to know their problems and help to correct their faults or mistakes. Be open to them and give them chance to make good decisions in life. Knock the doors of opportunity for your child and help them show their talents and skills. Teach them to be good and be vigilant in studying their behaviors.

Never break their hearts and convince them all times. Try to make them happy and praise them always to work harder. Be a role model and never act in a manner that is not appropriate. So as not to follow a pattern that is aberrant.

~ When they ask questions, their questions needs an answer.

~When they cry, their tears needs to be wiped.

~ When they laugh, welcome needs to be done.

~ When they are hungry, food must be provided.

~ When they need paper, pen must be provided.

~ When they want nice clothes , their bodies must be well clean or taken care off.

~ When they need help, attention must be given to them.

Help children and save their lives.

THE BABY YOU SAVE MAY BE YOUR OWN.

EDUCATE A CHILD FOR SUCCESS.

As a saying goes "education is the key to success" I quote.

Every child needs an education to be able to read, write and communicate. This is the biggest success that develops the mind and the body from ignorant or illiteracy. The world develops through education and Technology has taken its hand to the top.

Long, long ago there was nothing like modern education, talk less of its civilization. Man in ancient life was solitary, lonely and lacks many facilities to develop the world, but today we have seen a lot of improvement in man's life as well as his resources. The gaps of life has been filled with the demonstration of hard work that men achieved.

Thanks to our forefathers, who started this innovative creations. The children must be educated to help, serve and strengthen the fabric of the world. No child is born to be ignorant and skills must also be consider to make a difference in to their lives.

Before modern education was not known, the ancients use their brains to capture things for memorial. They transfer information from one generation to another through communication. This brought the emergence of education to our modern life.

Children have creative minds and that creativeness can only be shown through the help of parents or guardians. All children must learn to understand the reality of life. Every parents and guardians must struggle for life to achieve a good educational system for their kids or children.

Today, as the world continues to develop for education, many children are not enjoying this wonderful take. Some lack support from parents or guardians, others due to problems like child trafficking, child labor, child torturing or punishment, unwanted pregnancy, out break of diseases, violence against children both indoors and out doors. There are many, but to name few. These problems cause a lot of trouble and confusion in the educational system of many children in the world.

- What matters to children, must be a concern for the whole world.
- Their success must be our success.
- Their happiness must be ours and their great moments must always be consider forever on earth.

Development cannot take place without considering the future. This can be done through educating children to be professionals in different fields. Every child was born to fill a gap and they must be help to achieve goals. Educating the world needs a lot of help to develop the lives of people in all areas.

THANKS FOR THIS WONDERFUL GIFT CALLED CHILDREN.

Lets help children learn by listening to follow order or precautions, because listening is the foundation for every young learner.

MANY GIRLS ARE CRYING.

The world must consider this forever.

Girls turn to become women, They are mothers of the world, a sister, a wife and a friend as well.

Sometimes when I think of girls, it reminds me a lot, because they are the bearers of all children, the sisters of the world and the first teacher of every child. Women are more precious than anything, their eyes are brighter than the moon, when it comes to protecting their children, their minds are sharper than the sword, their help cannot be under estimated, O mothers of the world, their smiles are always a charity to their children, their playing brings joy to the heart, they wish the best for their children and their love is the best gift for a child.

Mothers cannot be paid for their hard work, but needs praises to be happy. There are many problems that women and girls face. Challenges needs to be overcome and people's lives must always be consider. Many women and girls are crying in private and public, or indoors and outdoors, because of problems. They are vulnerable and needs help as quickly as possible. The rape cases, the abusive languages, abortions, unwanted pregnancy, dropouts from schools, force marriages, prostitutions, cyber bullying, fraud, stealing, hunger and starvation etc. All violence against women and girls must be stop. Every man is created for good and life is not created for a mere play or enjoyment. The world must be safe for women and girls to live a comfortable life. violence must be out of every life. Every man must be a party to ideas that helps the development of women and girls in the world. This message must be put across to strengthen the nature of women and girls for the entire world. All deserves respect and women must be empowered in all good behaviors of life.

There are many hot tears flowing in the cheeks of girls every day. Who want to STOP that tears from flowing? Please help in anyway you can, the mind is versatile and broad, its help cannot be under estimated. Many girls cry of different problems and this problems increases day by day. The world is getting more risky every day. These problems needs to be tackle to help, save the lives of every woman and girl.

INTOXICANTS OR HARMFUL DRUGS.

THANKS BE TO THOSE WHO HELP TO SAVE CHILDREN AND ADULTS FROM HARMFUL DRUGS.

Many children are addicted with drugs, others are sick of it and some die in the cause, others in their dead beds and some in prison, who can stop children from using drugs? And who can save them from dying? Why are children using drugs? Who influence them to do so? Why not something better? Why can't some children make better decisions than this? And why some alcoholic?

These are sad stories that can make me cry and can make you cry and any other person who have sympathy for children. No child was born as a drunkard and neither was a child born as a drug addict. Please help in any way you can. If many children die of drugs or alcohol, what would become of our generation? Learn to help children, make them happy, allow them not to be frustrated, make things easier and confuse them not in decision making , Help them prosper and guide them to the right path. Rules are made to be followed, show them rules and regulations, bring peace to their hearts . Help them achieve their goals and guide them to do good. Mislead them not and never allow them to be in mess.

Please consider this and know that children have little legs and hands. They cannot protect themselves and neither can they create or make harmful drugs and weapons. The children deserves mercy and must be help to prosper in life. ITS TIME FOR CHILDREN TO BE HAPPY. They look forward to be protected and consider forever. Parents and guardians, peers and friends, relatives and neighbors and the world at large have potentials to help, save the lives of children in all corners of the world. Let every one help and take steps to help children successfully. This will make them happy forever.

CHILD PRISONERS.

Many lives are threaten every day. The children are becoming more vulnerable, something needs to be done , to help these children out of mess. Lives of children are getting more risky every single day. The world is becoming darker for children. This is the hardest part of children's life. Where are the parents and guardians to support the welfare of their kids. Hot tears overflow in the cheeks of children everyday. The child prisoners, what have they done to deserve this? Why can't we rehabilitate or help change their minds for good? Why not advice in some cases? Who want to become a victim ? Why can't we visit and advice them in prisons? Who pays the price to become a prisoner? Why can't we use another strategies? They need help in all ways, education, skills trainings and other useful things. Autism support is always needed. Imprisonment of children affects the whole world directly or indirectly whether known or unknown. These are problems that needs to be consider and care must be giving to them. It is a problem that the world must tackle as soon as possible for the betterment of those children out there.

Give advice, may be your advice can change millions of children in violence. These advises can be in paper works , posters, Internets through E-mails, facebook, skype, twitters, radios, Televisions programme, and other gadgets to help children from misbehaving. Advices are the best gift for thousands of unknown children on earth. An African child, Asian, European or any other continents , these strategies can be use to advice millions of children without seeing or knowing them. The governments, the intellectuals of all fields, the securities, the religious leaders and the world in general are working harder to help change the lives of children. Many are trying harder, but adjustment needs to be done in certain areas. Child crime is becoming too high every single day.

Sometimes its unbearable when children commits certain criminals acts and something needs to be done to save them from calamities. People must work together to develop the lifestyle of children in all areas. The world must say YES to children and help them serve the purpose of life.

Let the world cooperate to help children prosper in good activities of life. The children are very good, support their welfare. Every parent with children needs firmness in other to progress peacefully. Life is worth of living and attention must be given to every child. Parents and guardians must not neglect their duties or responsibilities and children must obey their parents to be successful. This is the best behavior for a good child. Responsibilities are made to be achieve and children with good morals achieves goals abundantly. Blessings are flying high in the sky and made for children with good morals. Respect is important to every life. Children must not cry and their decisions must not be contrary to good. Laws are general agreements that all must obey. All parents must be a role model to their children. A parent must not be an ill mannered person, as it can affect the behavior of a child. They must not also influence children to do evil, as we have seen parents who adopt children in a manner that is unfit for the society. Some parents encourage their children such a way that they can buy drugs, cigarette and other illegal stuffs for their children which does no good, but harm., others help their children to be prostitutes. Who are those parents? Are they helping themselves and their children as well as the world? Life is important and every child must yearn for good.

Good parents and government are not enemies to children. Every child must know his or her standards and limitations to be safe.

ALL CHILDREN MUST SAY, LET THERE BE CHILD PRISONERS, BUT NOT ME. THEN THERE WILL BE NO CHILD PRISONERS IN THE WORLD. THIS WILL SAVE CHILDREN FROM IMPRISONMENT.

Lets communicate with children to make them understand the language of life, because communication is the eye of language.

NOTHING CAN MAKE A HUNGRY CHILD HAPPY EXCEPT FOOD.

- Hunger a burden that overthrows power.
- A miracle that cannot be seen, but feel.
- A struggle that is difficult to overcome .
- A pain that a child can never bear.
- A feeling that conquers a child's life.
- Hunger, how hard it can affect children.
- It weakens the nature of childhood.
- An emotion that holds the breath of young children.
- A disaster that surrounds the world.
- A pain that is difficult to drive.
- Life, full of challenges to overcome

Hunger and starvation are major problems that children encounter in their struggle for life. It is an international problem that is unwelcome to every heart. This is an inevitable problem that surrounds the universe. Wishes and efforts are made everyday to eradicate this disastrous calamity. The government of all countries, people of all bar grounds are struggling harder to fight hunger and starvation, but despite of that fact, lives continues to decrease of its incident every day. Many people are dead and yet still many continues to die of it. Children are crying to survive and everyday hot tears continues to flow in the eyes of some children. Who is ready to STOP those hot tears from flowing? Why not help? How many are starve to dead? Who is the next victim? Who pays the price for this? Why sympathy is losing its way? Where are the people with soft hearts? Why are some children laughing and others crying? What can be done to help children ? There are many sicknesses that are affecting the lives of children, malnutrition, kwashiokor, marasmus, lost of appetite, Diarrhoea, cholera, stomachache, etc. to name few. These are some diseases that affects children, all related to food issues. Every child must have access to clean drinking water and good food to live a healthy life. Many children as well as adults die of hunger and starvation every single day.

Children are not happy with hunger and have less power to overcome it. Their crying must be a concern for the whole world. With hunger, life is difficult to bear. Help children to survive, as they need attention for better. They are our future leaders and therefore their lives must be well secure. They would one day take turn to care for our lives when they are grown, as the future lies in their hands. They deserve to live good.

- Imagine when a child is about to die for hunger and starvation, how painful that is .
- Imagine when a child is hungry searching for food, how sorrowful and sad that is.
- Imagine when a child starve to dead, how sad and painful that is.

- Imagine when a child gets sick for starve, how dangerous that is.
- Imagine when a child lost focus and not functioning well in school, because of hunger, how frustrating and painful that is.
- Imagine when a child lost memory or attention, how hard and confusing that is.

What are the strategies that needs to be done to help children?

Life is full of challenges and children must not cry. Children must be save from hunger. Riches of men must be use to help children survive, as they will one day take care of our future as well, when the age of retire comes for adults .Every child deserves respect and must be valued in life.

ANY CHILD BORN TO THIS WORLD, NEEDS HELP TO SURVIVE.

CHILD EXPLOITATION.

A child is born to be protected. Life was created for that purpose and every man must understand. The world is full of ideas and choices that must be based on truth, evidence, good attitude, self esteem, tolerance, obedience, Respect, having consideration for people, Giving chance to others and planning future for better.

Children are not born to be exploited and neither are they born for destruction. Many at times evil break in to the hearts of the teenagers, but politeness and steadfastness are the weapon for fighting evil. Consider your life and know your actions to live a safe life. Evil is not a title that promote heroism, this must be understood by every child. Heroism in life can be found through hard work and dedication.

Many people use children for different purposes, some for good and others the opposite. The children are innocent and must be use for good purposes only. A child must not cry. Frustrations and confusions have no room in the development of children. Manage your resources and time for the betterment of their future. Help them learn to acquire knowledge and skills. Make them aware of dangers. Plan good ideas for their development.

Child exploitation has cause a lot of problems in the world. These problems needs to be tackle as soon as possible to save the lives of every child. Many children are use for drug trafficking, child labor, stealing, prostitution, pornographies in both movies and pictures, frauds, recruiting of children to be come Gang members, Alcoholic etc. These and many others are exploitive methods use against children. The governments, the securities, and the public in general must help children for the development of the future. Every country is looking forward to its future and this cannot be successful without considering the lives of children.

Many children are suffering, let all work together to help them. A child is only a child and cannot take the role of an adult. The work of an adult must only be to save children from destroying their future. This must be understood by every man from every state.

OUTBREAK OF DISEASES IN TO THE BODY OF LITTLE ONES.

Children cry of many things and life is worth of living. The outbreak of diseases disturbs the body of little ones. Diseases are phenomena that conquers the whole world. These affects the lives of many children as well as adults . Many diseases are here since time in memorials, they are ancient and the same time modern. It is never invited, but the body always welcomes it. The body and flesh of man are facing a lot of diseases like HIV/AIDS, Cancer, Pneumonia, Diabetes, Malaria, Sickle cell, Polio, Diarrhoea, cholera, severe headaches and stomachaches, Liver disease and cancer of all types, Heart problems , Obesity, Organ failures etc. From East to West, North to South, the outbreak of diseases has conquered the whole universe.

Every seconds, minutes, hours, days, weeks, months and years, children continues to die of different sicknesses. Children are dying day by day and the spiritual nature of diseases are difficult to control. These are problems that affects every life, irrespective of who you are or where you come from. Diseases are border less and senseless. The government of all countries, Health sectors or department are working harder to safe lives. Children are very important and needs help to live a healthy life. The governments, WHO, UNICEF, UNCHR, FAO and other International organisations are working harder to help, save the lives of children.

The public views and opinions of child caring issues must always be a priority. Life matters and every life matters. All children must live the fullest of their lives. To have liberty, Equality, Access to Education, Health care, good food, and clean drinking water. These are the dreams for every child from every state or country. With access to this facilities, little by little the life of every child will be better. Children healthcare is a priority for the whole world. WITH CHILDREN LIFE IS GOOD.

CHILD CONFLICTS AND VIOLENCE.

Good attitudes make up human beings and when that lacks, half of an individuals life is gone. A child was not born to be violent and neither was he born to cause conflicts. Every child must not cry and that must be put in to consideration. People are created with a gap to fill and all must try to fill their gaps in a manner that is acceptable. That is why we have Presidents and Prime ministers, Doctors and Nurses, Police men and Women, Soldiers, Lawyers, Drivers, Pilots, Farmers etc. Every person has a role to play, whether known or unknown. Life was made in to the body for a genuine purpose that man must consider. Children are born with miraculous gifts, that when hard work and commitment is put in place that hidden gift will one day prevail. Children are not born to be wicked. There are many criminal records that children of teens have committed and these are examples that every child must consider to be safe. A child must not be violent and criminal records are things that can affect an individual forever. Give chance to yourself to do good to forbid evil. Every child must know his/her limitations and be very careful., For this will help children to hold a flag of dignity forever on earth. Be wise to know your choices and be good to achieve your goals.

Life is like a game , when you know how to play it, You are safe. Bright future can be achieve through hard work, focus, commitment, truthfulness and sincerity of the heart. Where ever you are consider your life to be safe. Make good use of your time and resources. Always remember that you are special and deserves to be happy in life. Never lose hope, for the future have many blessings. The more you try, the more you succeed.

WARS AND CONFLICTS.

What is the benefit of wars and conflicts? Why happening? Who pays the price to die brutally? How many die of wars and conflicts every day? Who is the next victim? How many becomes crippled, deaf, dumb, and blind because of it? How many homeless? Talk less of refugees, who flew to other parts of the world, lost their families and properties? Where are the soft hearts? This is driving the world to emptiness. How many properties are destroyed? And how many are stolen? Where are the good documents and certificates ? The world is weeping and who is there to make it stop? How many children die every day? How many lost their parents and loved ones? What are the number of orphans? And how many lost their hands, legs, senses etc. ? The children are trembling with the fear of conflicts. Every day is another page for different conflicts and violence that the world faces. Did this solve problems or increase death rates? Why is violence shaking the world? How many hot tears flow in the cheeks of children every day? There is no future without children and blood continues to flow every day. Many children are confused and frustrated. Lost of appetite, fear of wars, Injustice, Impatience, severe punishments, Imprisonment, poverty, heartbreaks, torturing , fire incidents, Diseases and many others are conquering the power of nature. The world is losing its prestige and the flesh and bone of man is tearing apart.

Power is not a matter of force, but knowing how to achieve your goals in peace. Absolute power corrupts absolutely and the wise knows how to achieve goals without wars and conflicts. Where there is power, authority lacks. The world must be ready to solve problems of wars and conflicts. Sadness and sorrows have overcome men. The blood that burst out of the flesh gets out of hand every day. These affects the lives of children as well as adults. Why are people suffering? The tense and breathlessness of the world is making a lot of hot tears flow. The blood that flows out of the body cannot be under estimated. What is life without peace? what can be done to save lives?

Peace and conflicts resolution must be a priority for the whole world. The world is created for good and its habitats deserves to be protected. Children are flavors in terms of humanity and must be safe for peace, progress and prosperity. The life of every child must be respected to live a happy life.

Wars and conflicts increases problems rather than solving. The limitations of life must be fully respected. If wars and conflicts solves problems, then there will be no more wars, because since time in memorials people have been causing or creating wars for success, but to no avail. The more it happens, the more damages occurs.

THE GAME OF OPPORTUNITY.

The world is versatile and a habitation for all. It is a land of peace, hope and opportunity for those with strong faith. The earth is spread across every part, with a sun that takes over the day and the moon takes part of the night, the sky above it and creatures on the ground , the night with its darkness and the day with its brightness, the trees located in different places, flowers with their bright colors , Animals with their shapes and features, Mountains with their firmness, Rivers and oceans full of nature babies, Life a miraculous gift from God.

The world is a game of opportunity for those who knows how to play its cards. The pavement is full of choices, ideas and opportunities. This is pavement for every child from every state, irrespective of whether a person is deaf, dumb, blind or crippled. Every person must work towards the development of these opportunities. The creativeness of man, makes life improve for better. People are created for different services which makes the world versatile. This showcase the capabilities of man in his environments. The job specialization of people brings development to the world. These are games of opportunity that men plays to Survive. This brings good health, security, access to technology, problem solving, understanding the nature of people, detecting of problems or issues at hand, having focus and commitment, such is life. The division of labor is important to every life. The game of opportunity demonstrates how versatile the world is.

A child needs help to choose the type of job he/she appreciates. The world is a home of opportunities and every child must have that opportunity to live a successful life. Opportunities are achieved through division of labor. "No man is an Island entire of itself". I quote .Teamwork, Education, skills training , and partnering with different people or groups are games of opportunities that emerges the rise of Nations and states in the world.

THE ROAD TO PEACE.

- Life, how good it is.
- The mind, how creative it is.
- People , how wise they are.
- knowledge, a miraculous gift from God.
- The world , how border less it is.
- The Oceans and Rivers how beneficial, they are to man.
- The Heaven and Earth full of signs for mankind.
- Freedom, how important it is
- Happiness, a miraculous gift that nobody hates.

Time after time, the world continues to develop through improvement of education , Technology and skills. These are signs of greatness that people have achieved. Every child must enjoy the sweetness of peace and liberty in the world. Equality is the idea of the sincere hearts. Every child needs equality to have a stable mind. This makes children comfortable and sound minded. Life began with a single soul and every man was created for good. This is the equality and fraternity that every person must consider. Human beings are created to be good and grateful, Think of the countless blessing that surrounds the world and be not ungrateful of the things you have not got. Appreciate the nature of humanity and have mercy for every one. The children are source of joy for the world. They must be save from Gang violence, drug addictions and trafficking, child soldiers of war, Alcoholics, frauds , stealing, smugglings, Theft, Injustice, Imprisonment, fighting, killings , suicide, disobedience of law and order, wars and conflicts, extreme poverty, hunger and starvation, etc. These are problems that affects the whole world. Lets Be a party to those who help people to do good. All these are problems that needs a solution and every person have a role to play.

The road to peace is all about problem solving and knowing how to deal with people and the world at large. The limits of life must not be cross and good things must not turn to bad. Rules and Regulations must be obeyed. Tolerance is what brings ease to the heart and comfortable is the friend of tolerance.

Do good to be safe and forbid evil to live a comfortable life. This is an advice for every child to live a happy life.

CHOICES OF LIFE.

Sometimes people wonder and keep thinking what to do. This cause a lot of confusion to many lives. Life was made up of choices. This choices should not be contrary to good. Every man is created with a sense of belonging which helps him to plan and to determine his choices. Such is life and man was created to choose his wants in decision making. This helps a person to decide, understand and know ideas of different things.

A child is born with no idea of the world's system. This makes many children vulnerable to many problems. Choices that are contrary to the law causes many troubles to the lives of children. This makes the role of parents important to be able to save their children from harm. A child must not be abandon or neglect, as they needs guidance to take steps to develop their future. This can be done through help from their parents or guardians to help, support, advice and teach them to have good morals. For this will help children understand the reality of life and also help them distinguish between good and bad. These must be the role of every parent from every state. Showing children good manners is what brings peace to their hearts and helps them accept good behaviors. This also helps the children to have a soft heart and to be able to make good decisions of life. Systems of the world is all about rules and regulations. These are settings that must always be put in to consideration.

The world is a struggle between good and bad, truth and falsehood, legal and illegal etc. These are all choices of the world that every person either choose the right or opposite. Man cannot escape choices of the world, that is why it is like a game that is either played roughly or smoothly to achieve goals. This makes the universe complex and complicated. What is life without choices, it is very important to every life. It might be sometimes difficult and sometimes easy, but such is life. These are struggles that man encounter in the search for peace. Liberty is genuine to the wishes of good life. What is good life? And how can we help children to attain the salvation for peace?

Every life is worth to have good choices in decision making process. But how can this be achieve, that is the question? Life is something that was put into the body to serve the purpose of creation. This is to follow good and to avoid evil.

Choices of life can only be proper if good becomes a forefront to every decision. This is what the people are task for, to be truthful, hard working, peaceful and supportive to all good actions.

SIGNS OF LIBERTY.

Liberty is a freedom that every man needs to survive. It is always a thing that hearts enjoy its feelings. When it lacks, frustration and confusion takes place. This is what every heart hates to bear. The burden of hardship is not a choice for any heart. The struggle for life is what emerges the rise of problems in the world. Man encounters a lot of problems in the struggle for peace and stability. These problems must be tackle for the resolution of peace. The energy of men are fading away, because of wars and different problems.

EQUALITY-must be a belonging to every life. Since the world is full of ideas, equality has a take in every thing. It shows respect, sharing and caring of people in different ways. It distinguish not and helps to strengthen peace between the poor and rich, etc. It is important for the stabilization of peace.

PEACE- It can be achieve through the equality of law and justice among people of all bar ground, irrespective of culture , race or religion. These helps to strengthen freedom and ease to the heart. It also helps to bring good behaviors to our lives and eradicate evil from the hearts.

LIBERTY- Is a freedom that every man needs. Every person must have rights to liberty, to have basic needs, sustenance and maintenance of peace to attain freedom. This will help, Make the world prosper for good.

LAW AND ORDER- This is a priority for every man to follow, for the sake of peace and stability in the world. Laws are bound to be follow or obey for the betterment of children as well as adults and the world in general.

These are signs of liberty, that can bring peace and stability in the world. If equality, peace, liberty, law and order are put in their right channels, the problems that man encounters for the struggle of peace will be solved.

A COLLECTOR.

A child is born with a gift of nature. Which helps them spiritually and physically to be able to search. This makes a child sound minded and creative to be able to do things. Every child is capable to do something, whether physically, mentally or emotionally to achieve goals. This makes a child to play a role in imitating what they see or hear. That is why every child is a collector of information and actions of both good and opposite. Sometimes you think they are small, but very wise. They have a good memory, which helps them remember things in their own ways. Imitation of actions, copying or studying people's ways of talking and actions, remembering what they see or hear, asking questions, complaining about things they hate, expressing their thoughts and feelings, crying or running away from things that frighten them, they also develop through emotions to have a sense of their surroundings. These makes children precious and important to the world. Every child has a sense of belonging that makes them intelligent to do things and capture pictures and information in their little minds. They need the world to help them understand the reality of life.

Parents and guardians have a big role to play in the development of children in search for liberty, education, skills, monitoring their behaviors or actions, giving them chance to understand the ethics of life, peace and tranquility in the societies and the world at large.

Every child has a role to play, when become an adult. This makes their lives important and needs to be brought up in a polite way, for the betterment of themselves and the proper functioning of the world. Children always imitate, that is why adults have a big role to help, save their children from calamities. A child is a collector of both good and bad. This is the responsibility of the parents to help children understand the dos and the don'ts of the society, to help them live a happy life.

RIGHTS OF A CHILD

The world was made up of rules and regulations. These are settings that must always be based on ethics.

A child is a human being with feelings that surrounds him. These feelings and emotions must be put in to consideration. All their decisions must be respected, if not contrary to good behaviors or manners. They are born to have limits, created to be truthful, protected to be save, motivated to be courageous, good morals to have a sense of belonging, encouragement to be hard working, valued to make them special, teachings to make them intelligent, talking or communication to make them understand , sincerity to make them generous, these are the instruments of a child's mind. To encourage a child understand the nature of life. The rights of a child is very important to help save their lives. Good children must not smoke, steal, arm robbery, fraud, accept bribe for evil acts, use of drugs, alcohol, prostitution, pornographies, disrespecting parents or guardians and people, neglecting of duties, disobedience to law etc.

These are not the rights of every child, because children must not cry. A Child is born to respect people, not to engage in fraud, stealing, accepting of bribe for evil purposes, not to engage in prostitution or pornographies, drinking alcohol and avoiding harmful drugs, not engaging in acts of violence killing and suicide. etc

The stop of this problems will help children secure their values and rights. Every child has rights to many things that the world must consider, but these rights must be inline with rules and regulations. All children must obey laws and order, for this will help every child achieve vision of hope and success in life. Peace and security can be attained if children fully understand their rights to do good and to forbid evil. This will help children not to cry.

ROUGH COPY.

Children grow up to become adults. From foetus to babies, from babies to toddlers, from childhood to teen age, from youth to adults, these are gradual process that takes a number of years. The progression of this helps people to achieve their goals. That is why children will say, when I grow up I would like to be a Doctor, Farmer, Journalist etc. It is about growth and the development of the body, both physically and mentally., to be able to achieve wishes of life. The world is versatile, full of ideas and opportunities. The chance to work, to have sincere heart, to be trustworthy, patients, travelling from one location to another, freedom of expression , Tolerance and obedience to the law and order. These are some of the choices that the world offers to humanity. The human right of every individual must be based on truth, to live a comfortable life.

The rough copy of evil actions are not good for children as well as adults. Evil must not be imitated or copied in to mans life. It is a havoc and brings destruction to the world. Many children are becoming fond of imitating evil acts, which are dangerous for their lives. This is bringing more threats to the development of the world. Every child have rights to imitate, but good. Children must put this to consideration to be safe. Good attitudes and approaches makes up life. being a rough copy does not make a championship, but being a champion can only be achieve through good morals, hard work , self reliance, self esteem and truthfulness of actions. Every child deserves to enjoy and this must be done in a good manner. Creativeness of the mind and truthfulness of actions helps children to develop their potentials. Life is very important and must not be waste for evil acts. Every minutes or seconds of life is expensive and must be put in to good use.

THE UNCERTAINTY OF LIFE.

Every day new pages are turn into our lives. From childhood to adulthood and from that to old age if possible, because not all grow to old age. This makes life difficult to bear, as people die every day both young and old. A person can laugh today and cry tomorrow,, another can cry today and happiness welcomes his / her life again. Some can be rich today, poverty takeover the next day, vice versa. some can be sick today and becomes well again, while others can be well today and becomes sick. some are born today and others die, some holds good positions and lost it another time vice versa.. Life is full of challenges to overcome. This makes it uncertain, as nobody knows what the future holds.

DANGER OF EVIL.

The world must be safe for children. Life was created for a purpose. This purpose is bound to be search. It is a blessing for mankind to search for good. There is nothing like good and it brings ease to the mind. Every man must have chance to understand the nature of life. Caring and sharing must have its place in the heart of every man. To help develop the nature of humanity.

Many things happened in the world not because of accident, but by feelings and emotions. Which sometimes are opposite to good. These are sorrows of life that must be out of mind for the betterment of the future. Truth is what brings ease to the heart. This is the joy of life. Men are creative and rational being, which helps them to decide. The world is full of choices, a division between good and bad, truth and falsehood. These makes life complex, because of the struggle between good and evil. Life is made up of options and every man must choose the best. Time was not created to be wasted, this must be consider by every man to plan for good.

The danger of evil cannot be under estimated in any way. As we have seen the destruction that is taking place in the world. Diseases has burst in to the body of man, talk less of wars and conflicts embedded in to the hearts of men, killings and suicide rates are problems that are border less, harmful drugs and smoking of different stuffs has already taken shelter in the body of many. Life was not created for evil, man must understand this to develop for better. The mind is broad and every deal of it must be rational. People understand the difference between good and its opposite, therefore choices must not be a havoc to any life, because life is only worth of living. Life is not created for a mere play, that is why roles must be rational to achieve good. No matter how difficult life may or might be, should not make people endanger their world. Every child must learn to be good. A child is very important and needs help in a conducive environment.

29

THE SUFFOCATION OF THE BRAIN.

Human beings are created with a sense of belonging, which helps them discern between good and its opposite. This is naturally set in the body to help people rationalise. That makes man capable of distinguishing the nature of the universe. Many efforts has been made to help strengthen the nature, but things continues to be complex and complicated every day. Drug dealings, stealing, smoking, Death rate of both diseases, suicides and killings, child prostitution, pornography , rape cases and many others are becoming more high every day. These are big threats to the world and are problems that dwells in the body of man. Some of this problems are far from over, because they continues to increase instead of decreasing .The life of children are at stake and needs help to be safe. All children needs protection as well as adults. These are things that must be a general concern for every one.

Many brains are suffocated, because of wars and conflicts that surround the universe. People are trembling with the fear of wars and children are afraid. This threatens the nature of humanity which cause the unlimited incidents in the world. Many are tired, brains are suffocated, some lost of senses which leads to madness. Every child must be safe from this calamities. Lost of sense, failure of organs, lost of dignity, focus and commitment are the most dangerous things that affects the functioning of the brain. Every seconds, minutes and hours mental illness continues to conquer lives in all areas of the world. The tension is becoming more higher every day and many are vulnerable. Mental illness as known to be lost of senses are problems that suffocate the nature of many. Every day children cry as well as adults for evil that is created/cause by man himself. Solutions are made to solve problems. Danger of evil has overpower men. Every seconds or minutes blood continues to flow, which has cause confusions and frustrations to the lives of many. Wars and conflicts has remain a scar into the minds of the victims.

These continues to eradicate peace. It is a destruction that befall the nature of man. An abomination that leads man to evil. Lost of lives, properties and families, these has cause emptiness to many hearts. Many are tired and their brains are suffocated. Pain, distress, anger, lost of memories, oppressions, sorrows and sadness has taken shelter into the hearts of men. The children are suffering and they need their lives to survive. The world is devastating and peace must be planted in to the hearts of men.

RESPONSIBILITY MANAGES THE FUTURE.

Life is all about being responsible, taking turns, making decisions, understanding the nature of good and bad, knowing what to do and being conscious of actions. Freeing of mind and being capable of taking turn in any given task. Self confidence and self reliance is the foundation for success. Adaption of these features makes life better. Every child's future must be consider, to help them develop their potentials. Help children take responsibilities and roles to achieve the best in life. Goals of life cannot be achieve without responsibilities. This shows the importance of responsibility in the development of the world. The future of every child must be good, for this will help develop the world for better. Proper education of children must always be a priority to help them understand responsibilities of life. Communication must be done to transfer information for the benefit of every child.

Responsibility manages the future for better. No matter how difficult the world is, responsibilities must not be neglected in men's heart. The world is in economic pressure , because responsibility is lacking in many lives. Dependence rate is so high and employment rate is decreasing every day. The chances of opportunity is fading away. Survival depends on fitness and many have no idea of how to develop their potentials. Time is expensive and the world is struggling for peace. Life is full of precautions to follow. Every child needs help to understand those precautions. Children are very special and need help to prosper. They are born to be protected and care must be given to them.

THE SORROWS OF CHILDREN.

*How many hot tears flow in the cheeks of children every day.

*How many die of accidents.

*Sickness or disease, how many children are in their graves, because of it.

*How many children are in hospital beds.

*From home to grave, How many children are there , because of wars and conflicts.

*Unnecessary abortions, how many lives are gone of it.

*Destruction of lives, how many has harmful drugs and smoking cause in the lives of children.

*Mental disorder or Autism, are devastating consequences that cause many children senseless.

*Hunger and starvation, the unbearable situation that cause many death rates in the lives of children.

The sorrows of children cannot be under estimated and the world must yearn for liberty to protect people from calamities. Every life is important to the development of the world. The children face a lot of problems in the struggle for peace.

The world must give hope to children to fulfill their dreams. The mission of children must always be consider, as they are born to be the future leaders. The world must consider this, to help secure the lives of children. No child is born to be useless, help and adjustment is needed for their progress. Their sorrows must be ended and visions must be fulfill for better. The good wishes that children have in mind, must not fade away, because of problems.

DICTATORSHIP HAS CONQUERED THE LIVES OF CHILDREN.

Leadership is an inevitable thing in the democratic system of the world. It was ancient and the same time modern. Leadership has been on and on from one generation to another. Success is a companion of a new generation. The goodness of life depends on the attitude of people. Leadership is a role that men use to lead one another in terms of protection and management of resources. The world is a home for all, with a vastness that is unlimited. It is border less and neither was it surrounded by walls. Life is created with unlimited resources, which helps people to improve their ways of life. These resources are abundant blessings for people in all parts of the world. All natural resources are created to help people of all bar grounds, irrespective of gender , race or culture.

Leadership is not a new thing in the world. It is an ancient companion of a new generation. People has

been leading since time of memorials. Life is created to lead one another, but not in the form of dictatorship. Leading is an important thing in life. Dictatorship is not a conducive way of ruling the masses. This has cause a lot in the lives of children. It is a social change that must be abolish to help save children from calamities. Many leaders becomes dictators, by leading in a manner that suits them, with no consideration of what people feels. Governing people must be based on their consent. Leaders are choose, because of trust that people have in them. This trust must not be neglected to cause disappointment in people's hearts. These problems of dictatorship leads the world to many wars and conflicts, which cause a devastating consequences. Today the world continues to face problems upon problems.

Dictatorship has conquered the lives of children in many ways. Wars and conflicts has cost many children their lives, school dropout rates become high, lack of proper education, Health care, insufficient food supply and lack of clean drinking water, some die of hunger and starvation, others becomes refugees with their parents, homeless, some lost parents in that cause, others lost of legs , hands, etc. These are some problems that conquers the lives of many innocent children. They have no clues or ideas of politics in young age, but always feel the agony. No Child is free in this types of conditions and every government must consider this to save children. Leaders are elected to lead as it is not illegal, but its rules must be respected. To help save lives in all cases. Government by personal ambitions is a dictatorship way of ruling the masses. People have rights and must not be seize from them. The children are born with gift and needs help to develop. The future must be safe for children and their lives must be protected.

MORALS ARE IDENTITIES.

Long, long ago, people were created with an unlimited resources. These resources helps them improve their lifestyle to be able to socialise and develop their potentials. Life is all about hardworking with a clear proof of determination, Through imaginative works with communication of sharing ideas through the improvement of modern technology. Life began with a single soul and continues to develop with crowds. Little by little many people are born to this earth with ideas and innovations. These emerges the development of people with their resources. A hard work that manifest the intelligence of man in his environment. Development starts with an improvement of ideas. Life is interesting with different qualifications.

The ancient people develop the world through the shed of tears and blood. Some of them suffered for the rest of their lives. They search for liberty, equality and fraternity. These shows the importance of the world and its habitats.

The world is not created for a mere play. Hard work, sincerity, religious tolerance, obedience to the law and truthfulness is the backbone of life. That is why morals are identities. Whatever a person do, will either favor or stand against him. Such is life and man is not created to cause harm. Ancient people are identified for their hard work and every other person will be judge according to actions. Every child must consider life to be safe. The world is unsafe for evil and peace must not be plan upon falsehood. The lightening of evil must not be allow in men's life. Whatever evil a person commits, becomes an identity, so as good.

What defines a human being is his morals and people are identified through their behaviors. Many people has gone, but mark the world with their records they left behind and others with difference. These are tokens or signs of life that every child to reflect on.

LET EVERY CHILD TRY TO BE AMONG THOSE WHO MARK THE WORLD WITH GOOD.

WHAT EVERY CHILD DESERVES.

Life is a given task, that must be achieve in a civilise manner. Every child born to this earth comes with a mission whether known or unknown. Role of every man is bound to be completed, to help strengthen the nature of the world. Empowerment of children must be a priority for every government, irrespective of race, religion or social setups . These values must be respected to develop the lives of every child.

What every child deserves must be a concern for the whole world. It must not also be surrounded by evils or problems. They have a role to play and nothing must hinder them. The problems that children faces are not a step towards development. Every child deserves to be educated, to have good food and clean drinking water, free from all harmful drugs, good clothing, Housing/shelter, Access to health care, parental control/care, free from wars and conflicts, free from child exploitations like sexual abuse and many other problems. These are what every child deserves to have, to be safe from calamities. The world must be conducive for children and problems must be solve to save their lives.

The chance of living is becoming more risky for children every day. The world must put hands together to say NO to wars and conflicts. It is in the hearts of men that peace can be planted to bring peace, for the safety of children and the world in general.

Every child deserves peace. Life is worth of living and peace is a breath that every heart needs. Liberty is important to every life. All lives are expensive and resources are divine gifts that must be put into good use.

LIBERTY IS THE FOOD OF THE SOUL.

The body needs food to survive, so as the soul needs liberty for freedom. It is something difficult to achieve as result of problems that man continues to face. People manage to escape problems, but to no avail. Life is important and attention must be given to every one. The children must not cry and the world must continue to help save the lives of children. The world is full of disastrous problems and children must be protected. The rights of people must not be seize directly or indirectly. The voices are important and every man must live peacefully. The destruction of the world are sorrows that leads man to danger. Trials and tribulations are becoming more higher every day. The moaning of problems are already out of hand. The dangers of it cannot be estimated. It drives many crazy and unlimited nature of problems cause a havoc to man's life. Peace is losing its route in many hearts and the joyous moments are fading from many lives. The world continues to bear burdens of different problems both directly and indirectly. Children are crying and many problems are driving the world to emptiness. Freedom must be planted in to every life.

Evil must be avoided and must not overpower good in any affairs of the world's development. Wars and conflicts should not be tolerated in the hearts of people . What makes men sad is evil and what makes them happy is peace. Every life must be protect, as evil brings no joy to the heart. The international system is based on relationship and that mutual benefit must be fully respected. Peace , love and unity must be a concern for the whole world.

INTERNATIONAL RELATIONSHIP.

There is something residing in the world, that tides borne together and the development of it cannot be undermine , it is social, cultural, and moral. It binds people together, to ensure peace and security. These shows mutual benefit of caring and sharing of resources. It is essential with relevant activities that helps to support man.

The international relationship is differently defined by different people, all arrived in one synonymous thing. This makes the relationship important as no man is an Island entire of itself. No nation can stand alone without help. This shows the collaboration of people in the international world. The children are part of this unity and must have space to be comfortable.

The philosophers, the Intellectuals, the presidents, the political scientist, the Educationist and many others have defined International relationship in their own understanding. This is an important part of human relationships. It is a system that binds countries together and give people a sense of belonging. News of happiness is the property of the heart. Many are living with problems that needs to be solved for the sake of humanity. This is a vital development that helps people to interact and coordinate for success. Distribution of resources and management of it is a priority for this relationship. This socialisation develops the international system both politically, socially and economically.

These are networks between people and its connections must not be break. These must maintain liberty among men of all Nations and tribes.

THE REVIVING OF NATURE.

The world is home for all and established To make peace between people of all directions. It is a surrounding that covers people from all areas. These are natural settings, which makes it real, because nature is always natural. The world as a whole is a global village based on the capacity to reward and helping each other in the development of International system. It is the international relationship that helps the world collaborate. It is the interconnectedness of people in business and the development of technology in the heart of the international system. This is the issue of socialisation that helps to manage the affairs of people in service. Life is created for good.

The reviving of nature must be done to help children live a better life. As problems are bound to happen, but solutions are always needed. The world must revive for better, so as to develop the lives of children from all areas. The wars , conflicts and all crimes must be eradicated for good. Children are nature babies and need attention for better life. The nature of their great moments must not be denied. They are special and the world must revive to make their future bright. It is true that peace and liberty are one and needs to be practice for the revitalisation of the world. This helps to ensure good security of people and properties. The lives of children can also be safe through this development. Life is all about planning for better, when this lacks depreciation of development takes over. Every child deserves help on issues pertaining to their lives. Children needs peace to be comfortable. They must not be distressed and needs a peace of mind to survive. Life is all about development and knowing how to plan for the future. Planning of future does not only mean knowing how to gather wealth, but knowing how to control oneself from evil.

THE BACKWARDNESS OF DEVELOPMENT IN THE LIVES OF CHILDREN.

Development is an important thing in the international system. It is what every country or Nation struggles to achieve. Trials and tribulations of the world is all because of it. Every country yearn for development, it is love by all and hate by none. People of all countries encounter problems, in the search for it. Many strategies are made and people continues to struggle for life. Children must not be excluded from this permanent interest . The life of every child must be consider for the development of future. It embarks on the joining of hands together to ensure peace, order and justice in the lives of children. The life of every child must be secure for future development. It is a system that must be done for mutual benefit. This also helps people to change ideas, properties and material goods to enhance peace and harmony in the lives of children.

The backwardness of development in the lives of children are cause by problems that the world continues to face everyday. The development of children is not going forward, it detoriates day by day. Due to wars, conflicts, child exploitation, child labor, drug addiction etc. These problems and many others brings no development in the lives of children, but destruction. Many problems are happening in the lives of children. Every day it increases instead of decreasing. Many becomes homeless, because of wars and conflicts, some lost their senses in that cause and others are now in the graves. And who is the next victim? Did children deserves to live like this? When are these problems going to end? No child pays the price to die brutally and what strategies can be done to save children from calamities? Every child deserves to be valued and respected for the development of the world.

THE PAIN OF LIFE.

As the world continues to grow older, problems of all types embedded in to the lives of people. Many children are desperate and confusions continues to conquer lives. The joyous moments are fading away. Weeping overpower men, the children cry for liberty, destruction of properties, unlimited wars and conflicts, danger continues to appear and peace continues to disappear day by day , increase of death rates, disease, poverty etc. Problems are conquering the world. Blood continues to flow and distress becomes part of human life. Sadness, sorrows, depressions, anger, anxiety, mental illness, diseases continues to make the world dangerous for children as well as adults.

Pain continues to flow in the body of man. Illegal occurring becomes a threat to every life. Frustration has taken part of destruction. People are tired and many are getting more confuse every day. Millions has flew away for problems. Refugees continues to become homeless with children. The demand for food and water cannot be under estimated. Prisoners of war are yearning for liberty. Contradiction of affairs mislead men from all areas. Aberration has taken a step in many lives. Children continues to annoy. The pain of destruction has damaged many lives.

No seconds passes without dead and blood flows for no genuine reason. Life is not created for this purpose and every man must understand. The world is created for good and truth must be the leader of every conversation. This will help save children as well as adults from calamities. Grievance and uncertainty of life has cause many conflicts in the societies. Sexual harassment and abuse continues to be aberrant and disturbs the lives of many children. Why is the world becoming more darker every day? Who pays the price to die brutally? Why happening? why happening? Why is cruelty overpowering the world? The world has a Creator and rules must be follow.

CHILD DISCRIMINATION.

Discrimination is the practice of treating one person or group of people less fairly or less well than other people or groups. The world is an unlimited territory that covers all parts. Children lives far and near from all places. A lot is happening to their lives and cause many distresses. The experiences that children encounter cause many damages to their lives.

Problems of children continues to rise day by day. As part of developing countries like Africa, the lives of children continues to become more harder everyday. Child labor affects many and dropouts of schools becomes rampant in many societies. The intelligence of children are no more considered in the face of hard labor. These problems drives children crazy in a psychologically way. Physically and mentally the lives of children continues to damage. Their emotional feelings detoriate . Children continues to weep for days, weeks, and years without peace. And who is ready to make children happy? Some children work for whole day with little rest and comfort. With no good food , shelter and no clean drinking water. Others work with no rest or little comfort. Some depend on their work for living, which is aberrant . Children must not work to feed themselves and neither should they be discriminated. The problems of discrimination becomes rampant , child abuse, assaults, yelling over them, Abusive language or words, Child molestations, Severe torturing or punishments etc. and many others are damaging the lifestyle of children from all areas. Many children are feeding themselves and their parents in many developing countries. Children needs to survive and must have freedom to enjoy. They must not be spoil and neither should they commit evil, but deserves freedom to enjoy in a way that is acceptable. Yes, we all know that children must be polite and live in a gentle life to obey their parents and respect people, but that does not mean they have to suffer for the rest of their lives. Many children continues to work even if they are not feeling well. Something must be done , because children are human beings with blood flowing in their veins. It is important that children must help their parents, but there is a limitation for everything. Blessings are for children who help their parents, but should not cost them their lives.

CHILDREN WITH DISABILITY.

Many children are born with disabilities, some of which are natural and others are not. Problems of wars, conflicts, fire incident, floods, Accidents by sea, land and Air are all forms of disasters that cause a lot of damages in the lives of children. Diseases also have many impacts in the problems that children face. Some of the diseases like polio and many parasites has cause disabilities to children of different areas, others due to incidents in hospitals becomes victims. Waves of sadness has taken over the lives of many children. This is the hardest part of life that many children continues to face.

Many children with disabilities are neglected and abandon by their parents or the societies, especially developing countries like Africa. Half of children with disabilities are beggars and continues begging for the rest of their lives. They face many problems and struggle for peace. Some continues in hardship with no or little education, skills and have no dignity. Sorrows and sadness over fall many with no chance to overcome them. They face many stigma and discrimination.

People are created to help each other and this must be a concern for the whole world. Disability does not mean inability. Every life is important and worth to live comfortably. The world can only be peacefully, if mercy is put forward in every action. Children with disabilities have rights to enjoy like every other child. They should have access to health care, Education, skills and other social amenities. No child with disability must struggle for life. They must not cry and neither should they be discriminated. Equal rights to life, liberty and property must be done to support them in all affairs. No child is born to cry and every life needs a protection.

BEHAVIOR OF CHILDREN WITH CHARISMA.

Children are born innocent free from crimes, smoking, using of drugs and many other problems. This makes them special and naturally free from problems. Children at childhood level knows nothing about life, compared to adults. Their lifestyle is moderate and good. Children are special visitors in the world with no experience. They are born natural and were taught through nurturing. They are easygoing people with less power and experience. They develop their lifestyle through observation of characters from different individuals. Imitation of ideas from people of all kinds. This is sometimes risky for children, because not all individuals have good manners. People have different beliefs, ideas, cultures, values and morals. Which makes it difficult to imitate. Many children have role models without distinguishing some characters about those individuals. That makes the role of parents important to monitor their children's behaviors. There movements and actions of doing things. A child must be studied thoroughly to understand his/her behavior . All parents must be very vigilant to help, Shape the lives of their children.

A child with charisma is an easygoing child, who obeys parent, respect people, monitor actions, polite in words and actions, good interaction, tolerance, having faith in God, cleanliness in clothes and body, Obedience to law and order, Hard working in education or skill training, being focus and commitment. etc. These are children with charisma and must be valued for the betterment of the world. Their goodness makes them a silent warrior. They are also children with character, who have power to attract, influence and inspire people with the qualities they have.

They are children who interferes not in crimes, drinking of alcohol, pornography, sexual activities, smoking, stealing, frauds, arm robbery etc. These are children who dedicate their lives to good. An abundant blessings are for children with good manners. Every child must be good to practice good and again every child must be good to achieve good. Every life is important and children must not cry.

THE RESPONSIBILITY OF EVERY GOVERNMENT.

There is no state or Nation without government. Countries are not anarchical or have no ruler and all have strategies to achieve their goals. Every government have their own ways or policies of developing their countries. The use of natural endowments, material goods, money and transactions of all kinds. These are the relevant and wisest part of international relations. It is about how, where and when to get things. These continues to awaken and enlighten people's mind in the business activities. Countries share and care to fulfill their aims and objectives in the natural world, to maintain balance of economic and social welfare.

As the affairs of children are always issues at hand, the government of every state or Nation have a role or responsibility to care for children in all conditions of life. The life of every child matters and needs help to be protected. There welfare must always be prioritise to live a successful life. The children face many challenges in terms of wars, conflicts, hunger and starvation, economic breakdowns, and many others. Which are all problems that governments must tackle to save children. These are responsibilities of every government to ensure development. A girl child as well as boys all need attention to see positive impacts in their lives.

These feelings, determinations, sensations and equalities must be part of every government for the freedom of people and their properties. Children must not suffer or cry. The major problems continues to overtake man in his environment. These are possible side effects that makes life difficult to bear. As challenges continues to cause difficulties in the world's development, peace remain wanted.

DEVELOP YOUR FUTURE.

As life continues to grow, children also continues to grow more fit to live in their environments. They are naturally born to take good steps in their lives, A good steps that will never fall and neither can it be damage, to have a long lasting happiness. Life is only worth of living. Every child must try to understand the difference between good and evil, to achieve liberty and become successfully in future. Life was not created for evil and this must be a consideration for every one. Every thing in this world is a division between good and evil, legal or illegal, truth or falsehood. There is nothing like peace and development on earth.

A child's life can only be develop, if hard work and politeness is put forward. The world is full of challenges to overcome, despite those challenges every child must try to develop his/her future for better. Many parents or guardians must stand strong to help develop the lives of their kids. Efforts are made for many children to achieve goals and those children with opportunities must try to put it in to good use, That is a responsibility of every child to honor. Every child must try to plan good and focus on it to achieve something in future. Life is a passage that every man must cross and these are responsibilities for every man to plan for good.

Man is created to be hard working and play his part legally. People continues to work from one generation to another. That is why every generation comes with its people to help, serve and strengthen the affairs of the world. This makes the role of every man important and roles must be done in an acceptable manner. Children have a take in this and must be firm to understand the reality of life. Help must be done to make the lives of children better and they also need to cooperate to make those dreams come true. Every child needs a development in life to plan for better future.

THE POWER OF CONFIDENCE.

Children are the future leaders of the world. Every generation adapt children for future development. These are the genesis of the future, they are the route that pave way for future development, an interest that helps people to decide for good, a chain that links mankind for better. These are the children that people must put forward to achieve good. The power of courage and determination is important to every life. Children are abundant blessings that occupy hearts. They are glad tidings of good news to the world. Life is all about working harder to achieve goals. Many lives are victims and needs to work harder for the betterment of their futures. The lives of children must be plan for good, so as to help them develop a confidence for success.

The power of confidence must be embedded in to every child. Confidence is the power that helps children develop their potentials. It also helps children to overcome challenges and make them determine to struggle harder. Every parent or guardian must help children to achieve something in life. This is what matters to the development of child's life. Development must be achieved through hard work and dedication. Every child needs success for better life. The government of all countries needs to put hands together to develop the life of every child, for the new generation to prosper in education, skills, moral and other useful things. Children must develop a good confidential system to help them prosper in anything they yearn for. Their aims and objectives can be achieve through confidence, hard work and determination.

Children of all parts must be help to develop their ideas for the future. Every child must be confident to achieve goals and must work towards its development. Life is all about planning and children must struggle for life, because one day mom and dad will not be there for you. All children must achieve something positive. This is the power of confidence, to be God fearing, good, vocal, hard working, determine and vibrant to be successful.

HOPE.

Another day, weeks, months and years continues to be inevitable thing in man's life. It is a natural phenomena that cause changes of generation. Every generation has its time and people. The life of every person counts to its development in one way or the other. The world is a home of hope for every one, irrespective of religion , race, culture, norms and values. The right to life is mandatory upon everyman. The chance of hope and opportunity must be given to every child from every state.

Hope is the best thing that gives chance for the development of the future of children . Every parent or government must give hope to children for the development of success. Many children are victims of different problems and need help to develop their potentials. The downfall of children are problems that needs a solution. The life of every child is worth to live, as they are young and need help to survive. All environments must be conducive for children. Their lives must not be forgotten in the world's development. Children are too young to face problems and neither should they die in the cause. All decisions must be a chance of hope and not a chance of destruction. These are problems that the world must overcome, to stabilize peace and development. The joy of childhood must be a responsibility for every parent and government. Children are extremely vulnerable to all types of problems and conflicts. The powerlessness of children should be a concern for the world to consider. Children are warriors by nature and needs improvement to develop for the future. It is very important to give children hope, because it awaken their senses to work harder and makes them courageous in life. These also helps them to be determine and give them comfort to act and react for good.

TRY TO CROSS THE BRIDGE OF CHILDHOOD.

Many live and die without enjoying the sweetness or nature of childhood, because of problems. Some live, but cannot make it and their doors of opportunity closed, some survive the agony, but their lives are meaningless. Many lives become a mess and they regretted for the evil they have committed.

A child is not born to be evil and neither was he born to destroy. Life is very important and no child should be a monster, even if you have the power or means. Never be a monster on the face of the earth. A child must be submissive to parents or guardians and people in general. Every thing about life is turn, whatever we do will either favor us or stand against us. These are real facts that surrounds the world. Many children die at young age, because of the evil they have committed. Among them there are some who lack support from parents or loved ones, others because of disobedience they cannot make it in life.

Every child must try to cross the bridge of childhood. These can be done if children live a life that is acceptable to avoid evil. The problems of evil cannot be under estimated and does not help a child at all. It is very dangerous and cause many agonies. No child should live in mess or die young, because of evil. A child is worth than evil and again I repeat a child is worth than evil. LET EVERY CHILD CONSIDER

THIS FOREVER AND ADULTS AS WELL.

Printed in the United States
By Bookmasters